# Leade

## *Sharing*

MANAGEMENT
POCKETBOOKS

# Leadership
## *Sharing The Passion*

Inspiration for business leaders on how
to achieve truly outstanding
team performance

**Jan R. Jonassen**

Illustrations by:

**Phillip Hailstone**

Introductions by:

**Helmut Maucher,**
Chairman of the Board, Nestlé SA, Switzerland

**John Tusa,**
Managing Director, Barbican Centre, London

**John Manger,**
Managing Director, Royal Philharmonic Orchestra, London

© **Copyright Jan R. Jonassen 1999**

Published by Management Pocketbooks Limited,
14 East Street, Alresford, Hants SO24 9EE, U.K.
Tel: +44 (0)1962 735573
Fax +44 (0)1962 733637
E-mail: pocketbks@aol.com
http://members.aol.com/pocketbks

This edition published in 1999

Printed in England by Alresford Press Limited,
Alresford, Hampshire SO24 9QF


ISBN 1 870471 68 7

British Library Cataloguing-in-Publication Data
A catalogue record for this book is available
from the British Library

# Table Of Contents

# Introduction

When, many years ago, I defined the leadership qualities required for a manager, I stated that credibility was the key ingredient for the leader of any organisation made up of human beings. 'Leadership: Sharing The Passion' has, if anything, confirmed my belief.

Any organisation, be it an orchestra or a corporation, looks to a leader for reassurance, for support, for guidance - but also for a challenge to make it go beyond what it believes it can do, to aim for excellence. Conductors or corporate leaders succeed by freeing the creative drive that exists in the best elements of the organisation, by letting these people stretch their wings and by encouraging them to try new angles and approaches. Yet, at the same time, leaders need to have their eye on the whole, on the strategic direction they have determined and on the goals they have set.

Freeing creativity, building trust and harnessing them for the good of the whole will not work without credibility. Only practising what one preaches will generate the conviction that the leader knows where to go and how to get there. Nothing succeeds like success, and nothing in professional life contributes more to satisfaction, motivation and commitment than the experience of working in an organisation that is at the top because it has managed to instil in its people the conviction that by giving their best they do the best for themselves.

As a music lover who has seen many of the contributors perform, I marvel how closely their perception of their task mirrors mine. Leading people, seeing them surpass themselves and grow in their task, is the most fulfilling thing a human being can do. It teaches and demands respect for others, it requires a passionate belief in what one is doing and it yields results that sustain and enrich us. It is a message that 'Leadership: Sharing The Passion' transmits with clarity and conviction.

**Helmut Maucher**
Chairman of the Board
Nestlé SA

# Introduction By The Author

Is there any way that business can learn from the world of musical conductors? A few years ago I travelled the world interviewing great, successful leaders in every walk of life: professors, generals, chefs, theatre directors, business leaders, sports managers and conductors. I was struck by the reflective and enthusiastic way in which conductors spoke about their core leadership challenges. I decided to learn more. I started my project while living in London during 1994-1997. With the kind help of agencies there I was able to make contact with about 40 conductors, and I interviewed 15. Each interview lasted between one and two hours. I asked each person the same questions, centring around the subjects you will find in this book.

There is no leadership challenge in the world greater than that of being the conductor of a major symphony orchestra, needing to generate the highest possible levels of excellence in the most competitive environment imaginable.

The unique challenge of leading an orchestra is that of communicating your particular vision to a group of 100 talented, opinionated individuals, among the most expert internationally in their field. The standards you are being measured against are not just those of today, but of the great performances of all time. If you fail, you fail publicly.

What I found in the conductors was a strong and profound passion for their work and mission in life. Going deeper, I found the systematic use of leadership tools and practices in support of that passion. It hit me: business can learn from this! Business needs a degree of passion. Passion is a foundation for successful leadership. As the great Danish philosopher Søren Kierkegaard said 150 years ago: *Passion, that is the main thing, it is the real measure of human energy. This is the reason our time is so mean, it lacks passion.*

Conductors use powerful tools of leadership. They have a clear mission in sharing their own understanding of great music with the audience through the help of the orchestra. This is not very different from the mission of business leaders. Methods vary, but they all work to satisfy the customer through other people.

Two musicians in the London Symphony Orchestra (LSO) characterised the great conductors by these words:

*They are the conductors who have integrity, they have a wider vision of a piece, they have innovative musical ideas, and they are able to translate those ideas to the orchestra. They have the psychological ability to make you feel you want to follow their ideas. They may not be the most technically competent conductors but so long as they are able to convince the orchestra, most musicians will give up their time for them.*

*His instrument in terms of music is the orchestra. There are 90-plus of us and he makes it possible for us to perform together and melt down our individual contribution, which is clearly set out for us, into a cohesive whole.*

Most business leaders work directly with a team of five to ten members. With new technology this span of control is likely to increase. However, as we are dealing with human beings direct personal communication will never lose its importance and meaning. As a business leader myself, I wanted to know how the conductors managed to maintain a close and intense working relationship with almost 100 people. **How are they able to instil into each individual that motivation and drive to succeed through realising their leader's ideas?**

Well, that's what this book is all about. Test it out for yourself; what's possible in music is possible in business. It's as simple as that.

**Jan R. Jonassen**
Stavanger, Norway, September 1998

# 1

## Create The Framework For High Performance: Purpose, Values & Preparation

# Purpose, Values & Preparation

*T*he success of any leader depends on the ability to create the right framework for high performance. Based on interviews with top leaders in every walk of life, all over the world, my experience is that the right framework principally consists of four elements.

1. **A clear, communicated and understood purpose**
2. **A set of commonly used values**
3. **A certain degree of discipline towards an operating system**
4. **The habit of good preparation**

Sir Colin Davis embraces that framework brilliantly:

> It's a commitment to a system. Total freedom ends in panic. You have to have your freedom, but freedom only really works within a framework, otherwise it isn't freedom, it's nothing at all. You've got to have the discipline of a framework, family, orchestra or whatever it is you're doing. Then you can find your freedom within that and you can find your strength and rehabilitate yourself.

**Sir Colin Davis**

# Introduction

The public perception of the 'great conductor' - or even of the not so great one - is of the (usually) male, wildly gesticulating, ego-displaying, musical director. When the players are cowed, the audience overcome, and the composer beaten into shape, then the 'great conductor' graciously, and in a properly exhausted manner, accepts the endless applause of the crowd.

Reading actual descriptions of the conductor's work, the gap between perceived reality and the truth is huge. Intelligent conductors not only have a strong sense of purpose, they also know that it must be shared with the orchestra. Even so, a poor orchestra will stop a conductor from realising his or her true potential. The moral is that the wise conductor has players who are the best that money can buy. If they are doing their jobs to the highest standards, the conductor - **chief executive** - can concentrate on raising the standard of the output still further. That is the real task - getting the best from the best. From this viewpoint, the conductor is the first among equals, not the 'great dictator'.

The conductor, though, is visible in a sense that the players - however brilliant - are not. The conductor takes risks: risks personal exposure, risks making mistakes, and demonstrates leadership in the most personal way. That separates the conductor's role from the players'. But the weaker the players, the greater the risk for the conductor. The risk may appear to be focused on the conductor; but he or she reduces it by sharing the responsibility for the venture with the orchestra.

The conductor leads by example. The orchestra expects leadership, but that leadership has to be based on respect. The conductor must be seen to be better briefed than the players, to have a clear idea of the overall concept of the music - **strategy** - and to be able to convey that knowledge and that sense of direction to the players in a way that makes them want to follow the concept laid out before them. The players are professionals in their instruments; they will not respect somebody who is an amateur. The charismatic conductor is one thing; the incompetent show-off is another.

The conductor in short has a **Vision** - to strive for the best; a **Mission** - to get the best musical results from the orchestras for the benefit of the audience; and a series of **Objectives** - to devise, rehearse and play a number of concerts that leave the audience satisfied that they have had the privilege of sharing in an experience of excellence.

**John Tusa**

# Purpose

A leader's purpose is to strike a chord in others, leading them to share their passion and talent, and so fulfil their potential. Actually making the journey is part of that purpose. You cannot afford to rest at the top. Numerous companies have gained recognition, become complacent, and have then been left behind by more forceful competition, because they have lost the inner drive to keep seeking innovation.

An important part of a leader's purpose is to develop and exercise an ability to anticipate situations, changes and the needs of others. Identifying the clues that lead you to predict those needs is the best way of helping to fulfil them.

# Purpose

*When you mention purpose, that really strikes a chord in me. Why are we here? What are we doing on this planet? What place does music have on the planet? The more receptive you are, the deeper you get into it, the more you will get out of it. The purpose of life, my parents used to say, is about giving. If you have been born with a talent, it's your duty to do something with it. I'm not talking about God. The fact that you are born with a gift doesn't make you special; it's what you do with it that counts. Your duty is to work and fulfil your potential.*

**Iona Brown**

*The purpose is to touch the top. I have never done a perfect concert. Probably it doesn't exist. If it does exist, it probably means a rather cold, computerised performance. I like to feel the strength behind the stands - as if people are having a battle to reach the top. It's passion. So every time we reach the top, it seems farther away the next time.*

**Daniele Gatti**

> *I think if there's any confusion or uncertainty amongst the musicians you can say goodbye to a first class performance. One of the prime objectives of a conductor is to make the musicians themselves feel secure in their performance so that they can play to their highest standards. The best conductors I knew when I was a student were those who could anticipate problems. They know when a player is going to have a particular problem or when there is a corner which needs to be neatly turned. Even from a distance of 40 or 50 yards to one of the most distant players, you can still make the orchestra comfortable enough to do their best.*

**Andrew Litton**

> To me, the basic goal is to motivate them to play better than they do normally - to forget about routine, make an ordinary life, an ordinary moment, extraordinary. I try every opportunity to conduct youth orchestras, and that's a fantastic experience, dealing with young people because they do it for love, not for money; in other words for all the right reasons. They are genuinely moved by what they learn and discover - all those things we often forget as professionals.

**Paavo Järvi**

> The job of the conductor is to time the performance so that everyone is at their peak.

**David Atherton**

*I think it's essential to have a sense of purpose every time you go out on stage, otherwise there's no point in being there.*

*My favourite early experience was my first professional job, with Rudolf Nureyev. He was doing a show on Broadway called 'Nureyev and Friends' which had one work with a piano solo and him on stage. I was the pianist, I was 18 and I was a nervous wreck. We were on stage waiting for the curtain to go up and you could hear the audience on the other side of the curtain. I say to him, as any nervous, silly 18-year-old might: "Tell me, do you ever get nervous?" He's leaning on the piano and stretching, and his eyes flash at me and he says: "Of course, you must always get nervous. There are people out there who have paid a lot of money to see you and you have a responsibility to perform your very best all the time, which makes you nervous. But you must learn to channel that nervousness into excitement." I'll never forget those words. Rostropovich was another one who would often say to me: "It doesn't matter how unimportant the concert seems, every concert is extremely important".*

*So it's an honour to have that role. You, therefore, get a purpose which is indisputable and irrefutable. It constantly renews itself. Every time you walk on stage you are bringing to life a work of art for an audience that cannot be replicated for people at home. Your sense of purpose is undeniable and consistent. You have to do the best job you can to make this work of art come to life in, as far as I am concerned, the most honest way you possibly can.*

**Andrew Litton**

# Values

Personal values are reflected in our behaviour. Setting an example and asking of yourself what you ask of others are probably the best ways to transfer a company's values to employees. People appreciate honesty, especially regarding a leader's shortcomings and mistakes. Nobody expects the perfect leader.

Being a top leader you will, however, never know exactly what each employee expects of you; they are all different individuals. What you see as details, others will judge important. You can never win that game, and you shouldn't. Promoting the main values of your company, and living by them, will help you and your company develop the framework needed to sustain direction and success.

If you ask people to develop
certain values, you first of all have to
do it yourself. If I ask for discipline, I have to be
disciplined. If I expect people to be prepared, I
have to be prepared. So the main thing is to work
hard yourself, and hope that people will follow
and understand that this is the way to
achieve something.

**Christoph von Dohnányi**

I think people appreciate honesty. I know some people who
are incapable of saying they are sorry or admitting when they are
wrong - and that doesn't gain respect from the players. Respect
comes from the truth. I think honesty is the most disarming and
powerful thing. Of course, I prefer not to make mistakes but I
don't fear admitting I'm wrong.

**Iona Brown**

*Sincerity is the key to communication; if you do
not genuinely believe in what you are doing or
saying, then the musicians and audience will see
through you immediately. I am known for my
enthusiasm and this is what I try to communicate.
Being sincere is essential for a good relationship,
and for me a good relationship with the musicians is
essential for a good performance.*

**Richard Hickox**

> *You will transfer values to others, above all, through fairness. I think every member of the orchestra needs to know that you are completely fair, you don't have favourites, you don't break your word - that you will always give them a straight answer, even if they don't want to hear it.*

**David Atherton**

> *A nurse who was nursing my mother said: "Iona, you have to love her enough to let her go". I sort of couldn't but I had to. She'd had enough. She was desperately ill. You have to let people be and you have to give. You mustn't want anything in return. The best thing is the giving. But you do receive, because giving is receiving. The joy of being able to show everything from your modest experience is very exciting. It gives you so much when they realise. There's a lot of joy and a lot of heartbreak. But that's life. You don't have one without the other. Agony and ecstasy. It's the balance.*

**Iona Brown**

# Preparation

Conductors prepare by working with the score well in advance, often years before the actual performance. Leaders tend to work on several projects at a time, but great leaders have an inbuilt ability to focus and concentrate at the right time.

Conductors go through their performance in advance to reassure themselves that everything is in its place. This gives them the peace they need to relax and focus. Consciousness builds up while they let the unconscious work. Business leaders have a lot to learn from musical or sports performers in their systematic approach to preparation. I'm sure you have experienced the calmness which comes from your own recognition of good preparation. Attention to detail makes the difference between success and failure.

Few business leaders I have met practise or rehearse, even before critically important meetings. They may think through the strategy, but practise, no. A meeting becomes routine. It may work well; it may be a disaster. Conductors never risk a performance without rehearsal beforehand. A lot of things can go wrong in meetings because usually quite a few of the elements are unknown. Rehearsing different scenarios will increase the likelihood of success.

Preparation is a constant teaching process. The conductor shares his or her passion for the vision with the orchestra. In business I have seen only occasionally the force of a clearly defined vision or goal being communicated to employees, with a passion that drives them into vigorously wanting its fulfilment. It's a question of being helped to see an exciting future not too far down the road.

Bring passion into business!

*I think my brain and my heart know each other pretty well now. I just know that I have a fairly patterned routine, which operates wherever I am in the world. I go for a run in the morning and on the day of performance I like to eat something - generally the same thing - at lunch time, and then little until after the performance. It probably sounds staid and boring, but you do have a routine, or at least I do, that sees me through. I worry about it sometimes, that maybe I count on it too much. I mean, if you don't, can't, have your routine you think: "Oh help, it's all going wrong", and, of course, it isn't at all. Because your body will cope with that, too, as it does with any emergency.*

**Jane Glover**

*I try to exclude any thought. You must try to open your unconscious - you must wipe away all the conscious things of the day, all the people you have met recently, what you saw, and open up the unconscious. That brings me to a very calm level. What I don't do is go through the piece in my mind - that would make me nervous. Then, when I go to the concert hall, I'm ready.*

**Christoph Eschenbach**

*I expect to have prepared things way ahead, but for a certain time you leave the piece in a situation where you don't focus too much on detail. Then suddenly you start polishing the piece - that usually happens over the last two rehearsals.*

**Christoph von Dohnányi**

*I go through mentally what is about to happen that night. Also, there's usually a dress rehearsal in the morning. So you are involved in the finishing touches. After that you stay in that environment. You avoid cabs and shopping centres with loud music. You are in a world of peace.*

**Paavo Järvi**

*I will always play right through a piece first of all, to compare what they (the musicians) are producing with what's in my own mind. Then comes the benefit of 50 years' experience: I can go back to the beginning of a long movement and will remember where the problems were and focus immediately on them. So I will say: "Right. Bar 5. The clarinets are too loud there. We need to listen a bit more to this. Let's try it out." I will try it, get what I want and I go on to do the same thing with the next. If I am not getting the right balance I will make sure one section listens to another. "Keep it down there. This is what we should be hearing."*

**Sir Georg Solti**

*In a performance, because you know you can't go back and correct something, the mental process tends to be more forward-looking. In a performance, if something goes wrong or isn't quite together, it's a moment in time, it's happened, it's gone.*

**David Atherton**

*The most exciting thing about this as a job is that conductors become like Bordeaux! The older they are, the more mature, the better they become. There's so much to be said for music and gestation. The more you spend time with a work, the more you understand it and know what makes it work, know what possibilities there are, and therefore are able to get the best possible performance.*

**Andrew Litton**

# Tips On Creating A Framework For High Performance

- Set ambitious goals, but look for involvement in establishing strategies to reach them.

- The best way to promote desired values is to live them. Act yourself as you want others to act.

- Consider making time for preparation and even rehearsal before critically important tasks.

# 2

## Getting All In One Direction:
## Focus, Communication & Trust

# Focus, Communication & Trust

*T*he greatest challenge of international business is effective communication. Lack of mutual understanding affects performance considerably. There can be no sharing of vision, no sense of direction, no collective channelling of energy. Finding the common medium of communication, the intuitive wavelength, will be a primary task for business leaders in the 21st century.

Next time at a concert, watch the conductor, watch the unspoken language between him or her and the musicians, and you may realise the immense power of communication without words.

‘The art of the conductor is to be able to communicate with the musicians and, beyond that, coax from them an inspiring performance. I've seen enough in this business to know that the difference between a good conductor and a great conductor is that the great conductor can make them perform as he wants and throw that inspiration over the audience. ’

**Sir Georg Solti**

# Introduction

Musical life is full of stories of conductors destroyed by orchestras. Some conductors were just ignorant; some were over-bearing; some were charmless and were rejected. I have seen one of the great names of the contemporary conductor's podium effectively cold-shouldered by a leading orchestra with whom he was guesting but whom he had totally failed to convince - musically - or personally.

Wise conductors display a panoply of techniques - usually no more than ordinary human psychology - to construct the relationship with the orchestra that is the prerequisite of success. It may be as simple as smiling at the musicians; encouragement ('stroking', as the transactional analysts call it) is a vital part of any relationship. If you always bark at people and never smile why should they give of their best?

Yet niceness and consideration alone are not enough. Sometimes the conductor must ask more of players than they may believe they can give. This may be stressful, painful and demanding. It may expose them to the possibility of failure. But if the conductor never tests the players, if they are never stretched, then they will never discover what they can really do.

Iona Brown's remark struck home to me: "To make people trust you, they have to know that you love them". Some years ago, I wrote of the characteristics needed to introduce radical change into a mature and conservative organisation: 'To change an organisation,' I wrote then, 'you must first show that you love it'. I am delighted to see that my experience as a managing director so clearly mirrors that of a conductor.

But there are things that an orchestra must do for itself. It is made up of some 100 players, organised into a dozen or so sections. Each player must listen to his or her neighbour, each section must listen to the orchestra as a whole. One of the conductor's jobs is to get the orchestra to listen to itself. No one can force them to do it. Doing so is a first priority in getting an orchestra to accept responsibility for how it plays.

Conductors are there to achieve the best possible performance with their players. Success is the orchestra's, not the conductor's. It does not come from performance indicators, it is not based on the number of correct notes played, the length of applause or whatever. Success comes from the engagement of the imagination; if a conductor offers the players an image of what they want to achieve, that may be more effective than any number of numerical targets.

**John Tusa**

# Focus & Communication

You need focus and attention to detail in order to deliver the planned 'performance'. However, focusing on details alone, or at the wrong time, will prevent you from seeing the bigger picture.

Leadership is the art of silent influencing. All those inherent and implicit signals a leader sends to spread his message and make sure it is understood can be mastered. It's a balance between silent encouragement and persuasion. Employees look to their leaders for signs; it helps when navigating the map. People are different; some may need a more detailed map, or they will get lost.

Over the years studying people at work, it has occurred to me that there may be no limits to human performance and achievement. The leadership challenge is to untap that potential both at group and individual levels. The leader is an intermediator. It's not sufficient to inspire the employees, he or she has to enable them to inspire their customers. Then anything is possible.

*I'm talking about training an orchestra which is not in the top level. You will take a passage and work at it slowly, and try to indicate where the key moments are, what they should be thinking about mentally. Often it's not an individual technical matter, it's their mental approach. Possibly the reason they are having difficulties in the first place is that their minds aren't thinking about the right things. They are thinking so much about their right and left hands that they lose sight of the big picture.*

**David Atherton**

I will never forget when I was conducting the USSR
State Symphony Orchestra in Moscow in 1987. We were
doing a concert which included Rachmaninov's Second Symphony,
one of my specialities. All during the rehearsal period I remember
feeling so frustrated that I couldn't converse with these people and couldn't
express what I wanted, except for gestures. I had an interpreter who I knew wasn't
conveying what I wanted to  say. So there was a real deep sense of frustration and
we got to the second performance - the wonderful moment in the slow second
movement when all the violins get the melody - 16 players - and they were all looking
at me, and we were suddenly communicating in a way that I hadn't experienced
before or since. It was a phenomenal experience because you realised that there
was something so much more important than all our differences - beyond
the language difference and beyond any other political
and social differences.

**Andrew Litton**

I like taking risks in
communication because that
brings out something
unexpected.

**William Christie**

In my very early conducting days, in Barcelona,
none of the musicians spoke any language other than Spanish, yet I
discovered that there was a way of leading, of explaining, without
speaking. It's very important to realise this - the fact that you don't
need your language. It's a matter of experience. You feel sometimes
that there is something very strong between human beings, much
stronger than languages. As you grow older you feel it more and
more. It's a kind of telepathy.

**Christoph von Dohnányi**

In your professional life you
have to be disciplined and
incredibly focused.

I have a good friend who
helps me with that [focus] - I'm talking about
the music itself. By playing, we build a focus in
which everything goes into a magnetic field.

**Iona Brown**

**Christoph Eschenbach**

At the end of the day, that's what it is
- a team effort, a game of soccer, not of tennis. We live
and die together. As a conductor, you are the leader, but you
don't score any goals, they do. Building a team is one of the
most interesting aspects of orchestra work, as well as seeing
the gigantic improvements in quality, and making CDs
where there is a tangible feeling of 'this is
what we've achieved'.

**David Atherton**

It's no good having opinions about music.
You have to have convictions. If the
conductor has convictions and is able to
transmit these convictions to the orchestra,
then they will collaborate.

**Sir Neville Marriner**

29

When you get individual strong personalities you get 'toes sticking up out of the bath water'. You realise then that it's hard to achieve a perfect ensemble with these people.

**Sir Neville Marriner**

When 90 people are actually trying to co-operate, the individual ego doesn't come into play.  The individual imagination, mental concentration, physical prowess, we have all that but we don't have the obtrusion of the individual personality because that breaks the whole thing to pieces. That's why playing in an orchestra is one of the most quiet occupations because when you are playing, nobody can talk therefore nobody is asserting himself above his fellow.  He lives through the experience of the music without intruding with what is called his personality.

**Sir Colin Davis**

I'm looking at them and I might smile. Then you take off, like a bird or like diving into a swimming pool off the top board! And the music takes over. It takes you and you are inter-acting with everybody. You must remember to breathe in those first few moments! Shoulders down. I met a Dane at the airport, a percussion player, who said: "We got used to you. But what was so especially nice was that when you came on to conduct you smiled at us!"

**Iona Brown**

*At a certain point you should be able
to detect that a certain note is too flat or too
sharp. That's it. There's no talk involved -
they would hate it. And at the end, when the
music begins to come together, you can still
improve the quality of what you do by using
poetic comparisons - I mean, rather than say:
"This note should be played like so ..." you
say: "This passage should sound like a ship
coming into harbour late at night ...." It's a
combination of technical things
and mental pictures.*

**Philippe Herreweghe**

*The majority of musicians will force the minority to take the right path.  You don't influence the masses, you influence the person who influences the masses.  In every orchestra you can immediately pick up on four or five people who are front-runners - and if you can get them on your side you will soon have the rest of the orchestra with you.*

**Paavo Järvi**

*Every rehearsal brings fresh experience. I try to be gentle but if a situation demands that I be strong, then I am. Sometimes I have in front of me a musician who can't do what the aria requires. But before attacking him I think to myself: "Maybe this morning he woke up with a big problem. Maybe something happened to his family or he's not well."  So I think two or three times before putting a musician into a deeply embarrassing situation in front of their colleagues.  I'm there for him, to help him improve.  But if I find someone who is being disruptive to my work then I have no pity.*

**Daniele Gatti**

33

*It doesn't matter how you may be feeling, you must try to take on the whole thing - give them the feeling that we're going to enjoy ourselves, that we're going to have fun. It's a question of thinking positive. If it works - fabulous. If it doesn't quite work - remember a sense of proportion.*

**Iona Brown**

*Musicians are very intuitive people. They can see through anything. That's why I don't think it's wise to play games. The minute you put on an image you are conducting a war between yourself and the musicians which will make getting to the truth of the piece even more difficult. So I would never act angry if I'm not. I'd never act happy if I'm not. Once people realise that they will take you at face value and your reactions and expression of emotions will be trusted.*

**Paavo Järvi**

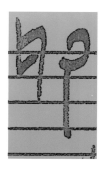

# Listening

The most important feature of communication is listening. I have encountered numerous business leaders who have the clear idea that the ability to speak well is the most prominent trait of a leader.

It is certainly true that you have to be able to formulate and present your ideas. But in daily life the ability to motivate others by listening to their ideas and giving encouragement is vital. A leader's prime contribution is to teach this quality by example, and instil into his or her team the ability to listen to one another.

*I am always prepared to listen if a musician, whether orchestral or soloist, has a particularly strong feeling of an idea, even if it isn't necessarily mine. But more often than not, because my conception is based on many hours of work and many years of experience, I must, of course, have set it into the whole. So I will explain that I do it in a particular way because it fits into the whole concept. And as I often say, you cannot afford to run an orchestra by majority decision.*

**Sir Georg Solti**

It is crucially important to listen to each other, whether you are playing or not. It must be of interest to everybody, what another person does. This creates a wonderful vision of chamber music. It's a feeling of togetherness, that the first violins are playing with the double bass, that the double bass knows what the bassoon is doing. It's so much more fun for people to play when they know they are with each other. Also, it's important that people know they should play more with their stand partner - there shouldn't be a war between them! I want them to play together and it happens.

**Christoph Eschenbach**

The sense of ensemble must always be the same. Basically the best orchestras in the world play well because they listen to each other.

**Andrew Litton**

37

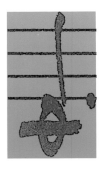

# Persuasion

Persuasion is often considered as manipulation. In fact it's one of the most effective means for leaders to reach their goals. As well as being able to listen, the leader has to master persuasion; otherwise unofficial leaders will rise to the occasion and use their own natural gifts.

Persuasion can require a creative approach in order to get the message across. Leadership is about selling your ideas.

American orchestras are often criticised for having lots of precision but no character. I'm determined that the Dallas Symphony will have both. One way I get character is by acting in an extrovert way, completely crazily sometimes, during rehearsal in order to get a result. In order to get them to swing once in "An American In Paris" I was dancing round the stage. I'm quite sure a percentage of them thought I was insane, childish, you name it.

But did it swing? Yes. Did I achieve my result? Yes. Do I care what they thought I looked like? No. They reacted to it and the result was positive, so I achieved what I set out to do. I will often do that at the expense, perhaps, of my personal integrity. But my primary function is to get these people out of their shells, to perform their very best.

**Andrew Litton**

*I have a million different ways of persuasion.*
*Sometimes I will do it by sheer force of direction, of clarity,*
*and by saying: "No! It must be like this!"  Sometimes I will*
*do it by cajoling - "My dear, why don't you try it like this?".*
*It's like the old Hungarian multi-cultural market places. You*
*have to have ten different ways of selling the same potato to*
*ten different people.*

**Sir Georg Solti**

*I think the qualities you display in front of an*
*orchestra have nothing to do with professionalism or*
*training or knowledge of the score. All those things will*
*help you eventually to get closer to the musical result you*
*want. I think the only thing that really matters in*
*persuading somebody else to follow you is your ability to*
*convince people that they should try things your way.*

**Paavo Järvi**

*I think it's a question of showing respect to the orchestra. It's a duty for me, not for the orchestra. I cannot claim the orchestra's respect unless I first of all respect them. And that means arriving prepared. How can they respect me if I am the kind of conductor who breaks this respect by being less than well prepared? And I am not here to lose time, either.*

**Daniele Gatti**

*The ability to persuade others
is of crucial importance. An orchestral
conductor should be able to sell
ice-cream to Eskimos.*

**William Christie**

*It's fundamental. Don't ask me how I have this ability.
You can see that the ability is there because I manage to obtain what
I want. At the same time as they are inspired, they follow someone. And
persuasion is hidden in that. Probably you want to use the word 'convinced'.
This is different. I'm not interested whether the orchestra is convinced
or not. The most important thing is that all follow along.*

**Daniele Gatti**

# Trust

Gaining trust is the foundation of leadership. It's the difference between formal administration and natural leadership. You can administer without trust for some time, but you cannot achieve results unless you can mobilise forces towards ambitious goals. This is founded on trust.

Your ability as a leader to convey the importance of the goals, and your willingness to involve the team in forming the strategies to reach them, are critical success factors in building trust. Once you have a level of general trust you have the foundation for all future success.

However, be aware that it's much easier to break trust than to establish it.

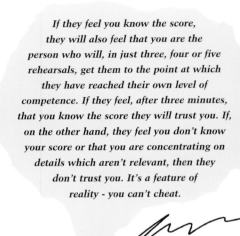

*If they feel you know the score, they will also feel that you are the person who will, in just three, four or five rehearsals, get them to the point at which they have reached their own level of competence. If they feel, after three minutes, that you know the score they will trust you. If, on the other hand, they feel you don't know your score or that you are concentrating on details which aren't relevant, then they don't trust you. It's a feature of reality - you can't cheat.*

**Philippe Herreweghe**

*To get people to trust you they have to know you love them. You can say anything. How do you make people trust you? Well, all you can do is to prove to them that you are trustworthy.*

**Iona Brown**

*Always consult them about this and that, ask them if they have another suggestion if something isn't working - it just shows that you respect them and that they can trust you for doing that.*

**Jane Glover**

*One has got to be so careful, to have great discipline through one's life to learn to keep one's mouth shut. Let me put it another way. The whole journey of one's life, when you have to work so closely with other people, is to try to get your ego out of the way. Most of the problems arise from the problem of the ego. If you allow your ego to take over you are going to make mistakes, you are going to get it all wrong. The perpetual erosion of the ego is the way forward. The rest will then declare itself.*

**Sir Colin Davis**

45

*Trust is built up over a period of time through shared experience. When an orchestra knows that you won't let them down (even though you've asked them for a lot of crazy things during rehearsal) and you know how to make it work, that's how trust is built up. Trust also comes when you make a controversial decision, say, in personnel or seating in the orchestra; when it works out people will believe you the next time. It's a long process or it can happen right away.*

**Andrew Litton**

*Of course, I sometimes have to carry out this unpleasant task of firing people. It's an awful business, having to look into a person's eyes and tell them they're no good, or not as good - but the one thing which has saved me from any animosity is the goal of the orchestra, the quality of the orchestra: if you are able to explain that, and I can, then you don't need to have a fight with anyone.*

**Christoph Eschenbach**

# Tips To Gain Trust

- Involve your team members and show them that you really respect them.

- Demonstrate genuine competence in the area concerned, and your ability will be recognised and trusted.

- Be supportive; make it clear you will not let people down.

- Signal the link between the company's goals and your own decisions and actions.

# 3 Intensity & Energy

# Intensity & Energy

*I*ntensity and detachment (relaxation) are like ivory and ebony. You cannot think of one without the other. Studies show that successful top leaders refer to these two processes as the foundation of their energy.

❝Intensity has everything to do with reaching a certain level. It's another word for energy. Mental energy pushes everything.❞

**Paavo Järvi**

# Introduction

Whatever the area of management, passion without direction is so much wasted effort. In any group endeavour, the interaction between the perceived leader and those being led must be both sensitive and dynamic.

Conducting an orchestra is perhaps the most intensely public expression of 'people management' that there is; one man or woman must convey to around 100 experienced and opinionated musicians exactly what the coherent vision of the performance must be, and must then ensure that that vision is brought to life in an instant. Because a live performance involves so many variables and, therefore, pitfalls, the possibilities of catastrophe and humiliation must always be present at some level in the performers' minds.

Many conductors acknowledge that the act of performance itself fills them with energy - not altogether surprising given that bodily energy derives from the secretion of adrenaline. Clearly, fear, anticipation, love for the music or even love of oneself can stimulate an adrenaline surge. All these are powerful emotions, and yet on stage the performers have to undertake a whole series of acts of supreme coolness and discipline. In the final analysis the head must rule the heart but the conflict itself is energising.

But, in both performance and rehearsal, a conductor must exude intensity and passion while at the same time motivating and enabling a group of individuals who may profoundly detest him or her, may disagree violently with his or her view of the music or, worse still, be entirely indifferent to their very existence. A conductor, like any successful manager, must overcome all these levels of resistance and carry forward a sense of vision to everyone involved - if necessary ignoring the most stubborn of 'opponents' in the orchestra. All this in front of a critical audience of thousands, who think they could do the job just as well!

Many, if not most, people would freeze in such circumstances but performing artists of all kinds must respond actively to performing conditions - and it is this that marks them out. Intensity means, among other things, the ability to concentrate, to shut out all extraneous factors, and channel all one's energy to the task in hand. Exactly what would be said, for example, of any athlete.

It has often been said that the truly great conductors are the type of people who would succeed in any chosen field. Perhaps that is not so surprising.

**John Manger**

# Intensity & Energy

It is not humanly possible to be intense all the time. After the extreme
concentration and almost total release of energy during a performance, whether in
arts or in business, you have to relax and recharge your batteries. Intensity is,
however, the most effective way of channelling your energy, like a laser beam, to
achieve the most demanding goals.

Your brain is the primary source of human energy. If you're aware of the potential,
you can create enough energy yourself even to withhold illness. The energy is there
all the time. The key is to unlock it, to direct it where it contributes the most. The
challenge for the leader is to create an environment in which each individual is
enabled to release his or her energy at the highest levels, at the right time.

*I think you must leave the orchestra with an edge of nervous tension before the performance begins. I think if you put your foot on the stage in an over-confident and blasé way you are going to give a blasé performance. You need an edge of excitement.*

**Sir Neville Marriner**

*I save my intensity for the performance. Two positive comments that have been made about me thrill me more than anything else. One is: "My goodness, you let us play". The second is: "You have such a sense of architecture". Your job as conductor, when you get to performance, is to create an environment which enables the players to play the best they possibly can and create the shape of that work, whatever that may be. If you can create that architecture, that's something which achieves a great performance, and that's where I channel my intensity.*

**Andrew Litton**

*I think the conductor and musicians have to create intensity all the time. Intensity and tenseness are two different things. Music is such a short-lived thing - it only lasts for perhaps 10 or 20 or 40 minutes - and in that time one should do everything to make it live. It's like life. One lives only a certain time, and then it's gone, so one should also put into life all the intensity one has.*

**Christoph Eschenbach**

*There has to be that wonderful balance between being totally intense and totally relaxed. In an ideal world you get over the intensity in rehearsal and then in performance you just release it, so everybody feels they are flying.*

**Jane Glover**

*Certainly, I get energy from the players. It's not just the conductor galvanising the players, it can sometimes be the other way round. It's like everybody - on different days they can feel different. You might feel terrible, you may have a headache after only three hours' sleep, but nobody will make allowances. You have to perform and sometimes you can be energised within five seconds - an energy which will last for four hours.*

**David Atherton**

*Physically you can be as worn out as a shoe with holes but you walk out on stage in the knowledge that you are about to perform this great piece and you believe in everything you do. I don't perform anything I don't believe in. That's what gives you the energy.*

**Andrew Litton**

*In my enthusiasm and intensity I will very often push people to the limits of their capabilities - and that must entail a certain degree of risk, emotionally, physically and otherwise. The great thing is that the risk pays off when that person suddenly finds something in themselves they didn't know was there.*

**Sir Georg Solti**

*Intensity is, I think, one of the basic ingredients to reach a superior performance. If there is no intensity in what you are doing, it is all flat and there is no wind to tighten the sails.*

**Sir Colin Davis**

*I try to be in control and out of control at the same time!*

**Daniele Gatti**

It's quite interesting, for instance,
that if you have a streaming cold,
and before the performance you are
absolutely full of it, you can go out onto
the platform and not blow your nose once.
One's body is quite extraordinary because it
has its own way of dealing with a crisis,
however large or small. I mean, you feel
you may throw up but actually you don't!
If you think you're going to make it, you
probably will, because your body
will look after you.

**Jane Glover**

*Every person is born with individual characteristics, with their own qualities. You need to be physically and technically very well prepared. You need to extract excitement from your players. That means your intensity must be everywhere, enjoying every moment when you are doing things. But the technicalities mustn't be seen, your hard work mustn't be seen, you have to exercise control. Intensity must be kept in check and precise direction must be given for every part of the score.*

**Neeme Järvi**

*I create energy in many different ways,
but basically by encouraging. I do this, especially
towards the end of recording sessions. I like to exemplify by
telling stories about when I made The Ring, for example, how Birgit
Nilsson would have sung the closing scene of Götterdämmerung
three different times, waiting for the orchestra to warm up, and she
would say: "No, I can't do it any more". And I would say: "Come
on, my dear. You can, you can". This was the extraordinary thing
about her: the final takes of the day were nearly always the ones
that went on the record because she would summon up reserves
that maybe she didn't believe were there.*

**Sir Georg Solti**

*In my case, it's my love of the music. I generally can't wait to start. If I'm tired, if I'm exhausted or sad or depressed, for whatever reason, I escape into the music, I force my mind onto the music. Once it has started I try to block out other things. We're all human, we're all in the same boat, we all want the same things - love, respect, affection, security, success, fulfilment, excitement, understanding. When I am conducting and I have a sea of faces in front of me, that has a huge impact on me. It's not a feeling of wanting to tell them what to do and they obey. They are waiting and I am thrilled that I am in a position where I can give them something that will enable us all to go on this journey.*

**Iona Brown**

*As a conductor you are not actually singing and playing yourself, other people are, and you are there to help them perform. At the same time, you've got to energise the whole orchestra. It is a question of being outside, of listening very hard to what is happening and at the same time being in it so that you can give the intensity.*

**Sir Colin Davis**

My experience is that not one performer wants to go on stage and perform badly. They all want to be part of a successful enterprise. If you can generate this confidence, that they are going to be part of an event, then even if they've had a bad flight and a rotten journey getting to the concert hall and their hotel isn't up to scratch, they still want to perform. They have the confidence to know that they are exceptional, that they will perform to a high standard and they know that competitively they are very much on top. That gives them energy. But the potential has to be there, and most musicians know what their potential is.

**Sir Neville Marriner**

I believe, particularly with great musicians that I'm able to collaborate with, that the sky should be the limit. And therefore as I am prepared to take the risks and shoot for the limit, then why shouldn't they follow?

**Sir Georg Solti**

63

> Energy has a lot to do with inspiration, passion and tolerance.
> You have to let people have their space and be different, sometimes
> extremely so. And you have to assume that their problems are just as great,
> even greater perhaps, than your own. It's important to be aware if any
> specially difficult things have happened to any individual - I think that's
> very important. To be compassionate. I have no time for pity. No one wants
> to be pitied. But people do need to be understood. There's a big
> difference between pity and compassion. So energy comes
> from their needs, in a way.

**Iona Brown**

> Why do some people have more energy than others?
> I can't explain it. Too many people get themselves so tied up with
> complex and mental blockages that a great deal of energy that they
> have is not available to them. That's when you get somebody so
> amazing like Mozart who obviously had total access to his energy,
> otherwise he couldn't possibly have done what he did. I suppose it isn't
> where does the energy come from, because it's there, but it's tapping it,
> that's the key word. You need to direct it.

**Sir Colin Davis**

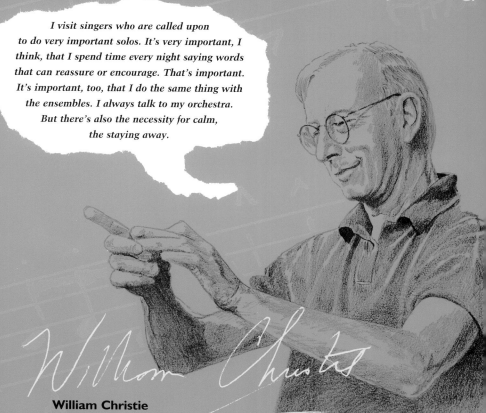

> *I visit singers who are called upon to do very important solos. It's very important, I think, that I spend time every night saying words that can reassure or encourage. That's important. It's important, too, that I do the same thing with the ensembles. I always talk to my orchestra. But there's also the necessity for calm, the staying away.*

**William Christie**

# Tips On Building & Releasing Intensity & Energy

- Focus your energy like a laser beam of intensity.

- Identify the right buttons to push which release the flow of energy.

- Your brain is the primary source of energy - use it to stay on top as a performer.

- Your leadership challenge is to create a climate where people naturally release and rebuild their energy.

# 4

## Keeping The Balance:
## Recharging The Batteries

# Recharging The Batteries

*L*eaders who consistently perform at a high level of intensity need to use techniques to preserve and rebuild lost energy. Some conductors have the ability to shift their energy to different levels and be able to step up their performance without wearing out, or even being tired!

> Well, I think that's something that you learn and it comes with what you call maturity and age, that you get some kind of balance going.

**Sir Colin Davis**

*Colin Davis*

# Introduction

The intensity with which any team leader must work will be both closely monitored by the team, and more obvious to the team members than the team leader. For a conductor, the risks of failure are high; he may lose the respect of the players, the attention of the audience, the thread of the music or, indeed, his career. So, when a conductor loses the edge to his or her performance, this must never appear to be the case! In common with almost any public figure, be they a politician, an athlete, or a high-profile chief executive, conductors must exude energy, passion and commitment, even if the battery reserves are on 'empty'. For any one audience, this may be the conductor's one chance to communicate and any great conductor will want to do that.

So, how do conductors attain suffient reserves of energy to be able to bring that required intensity to any and every performance they give? Not surprisingly, there are many different answers: Sir Colin Davis and Richard Hickox provide perhaps the most humane response, namely that they derive their strength and peace of mind from their family life. Other conductors find solace in the companionship of other musicians, and yet others in pursuing pastimes which are totally unrelated to their work. In these ways, conductors are just the same as the rest of us; they need a break from the exposure their work demands, a change of pace, or even a total abstinence from the high-risk public platform they inhabit.

As we have already seen, however, many conductors derive energy from the performance itself, but they certainly could not sustain that level or quality of intensity for any length of time. Indeed, anyone who has attempted a coherent conversation with a conductor immediately after a concert is over will be able to attest to the virtually total collapse of an otherwise fully healthy and physically fit human being. The need for physical as well as mental fitness is paramount given that physical fitness will enhance mental stamina. Many middle and senior managers spend much time and money on 'fitness regimes'; interesting, therefore, that conductors by and large lead longer and more productive lives than many managers without resorting to gymnasia and the like. Perhaps the emotional charge and intellectual satisfaction conductors can derive from their work are their own source of energy and their own means of release.

Whatever the reason, a conductor's work involves, in a much more concentrated form, the kind of mental and physical stamina, concentration and risk-taking common to many mangers. However, for conductors, both the risks and rewards can be extreme; communication failure, loss of trust and respect during a live performance of a complex work can lead to total disaster.

**John Manger**

# Keeping The Balance

Shifting between different types of tasks activates different areas of the brain and enables further activity even when recharging. For example, if you work with economics, mathematics or technical subjects you could expand your performance by switching to music, arts or creative challenges to activate other areas of the brain.

*Recharging the batteries has nothing whatsoever to do with relaxation in terms of boredom. One can recharge the batteries, let go and relax, but be very awake in the head. In other words, you can recharge at one level and shift the tension of life to another level. I think if you work with the emotional or musical part of the head, you have also to get the other part of your brain working, because music has also to do with numbers, strictly and mathematically so. Conversely, mathematics is not such a cold science. It has to do with philosophical things, which touch the whole human existence. This brings you back into human emotions. It's very much an interplay. When I say I can recharge my batteries at one level and have another level still working, that means I have many batteries! And therefore, actually, I am never tired - because I shift my energy constantly.*

**Christoph Eschenbach**

*Recently I was on tour and did four concerts of the same piece in a row. If I have a day off between, say, the second and third performances as I had on that tour, the performance after the day off is inevitably better. It's not so much to do with detachment but with re-winding the tape. Because if you are in the process you are constantly going forward. But if you have a moment to reflect, you re-play and you look at it from a different point of view.*

**Paavo Järvi**

# The Impact Of Family & Friends

My experience after years of interviewing high performing top leaders leads me to the conclusion that a supportive network of family and friends is the single most important factor in recharging human batteries. Family and friends supply external confidence and support, as well as the oasis needed to re-energise and build up.

*I have some wonderful friends
in the orchestra and once you start to
make music together the musicians will
follow and try to support me. I think it
would be inhuman to have a profession
where you don't make friends. It
wouldn't be good. If you can't keep
discipline while keeping friends, you
should check what's wrong.*

**Christoph von Dohnányi**

*I was taught from a very early age some very important things, not just about music. "The sort of musician you become will depend on how you develop as a person," I was told. "So you'd better be interesting, Iona. You'd better look outwards. Don't go 'me, me, me'. Go to galleries, read books, go for walks, go to the theatre, have friends who are not necessarily musicians." Most of my close friends are not musicians. I think it's terribly important to have a broad outlook and to be able to understand all sorts of different things. Tolerance is essential. People are fascinating and incredible. The human race at best is so miraculous. At worst, it's equally appalling.*

**Iona Brown**

*In my orchestra I have people to whom I am very close socially. I don't consciously differentiate between the orchestra and my other friends. But there is a degree of caution because of the difficult decisions one is sometimes forced to make. If you are too close to people your objectivity goes out of the window. The picture is distorted by personal feelings which ultimately isn't fair to the organisation as a whole.*

**Paavo Järvi**

*I often mix with people who are not musicians. I think the music world can become almost over-bearing. If you wanted to, you could spend 16-18 hours every day immersed in music and nothing else. But it's important that you live, that you know what's going on in Bosnia, what Bill Clinton's doing, what's happening in Chile. I love current affairs, I get passively quite involved in politics.*

**David Atherton**

# The Impact Of Family & Friends

*My family is the basis from which I go out into the world. If I didn't have it, I would feel lost and rootless and I would ask myself what the hell I was doing all this on my own for. I think one needs family and stability. It is enormously important. For me the family is everything.*

**Sir Colin Davis**

*My family and friends mean a great deal to me; when they are in the audience I make an extra special effort and they inspire me to give my best performance.*

*The funniest thing about this topic of leadership is if you want to find out how bad you are as a leader, have a child. They never do anything you want them to! You may pride yourself on your leadership qualities as a conductor, but as a father .....?*

**Richard Hickox**

**Andrew Litton**

# Tips On Keeping The Balance Of Life

- Find out which kind of stimuli refill your batteries and make you feel good. Remember those stimuli whenever you feel tired.

- Concentrate on each subject in your work for a limited time. Then shift to another type which activates a different part of your brain from rational to creative and emotional.

- Value time with your family and friends. It's one of your critical success factors at work!

# 5

## Reflections:
How To Stay Successful & When To Change

# How To Stay Successful & When To Change

**S**ir Georg Solti, in his quote below, sets the ultimate standard of personal improvement. There is always potential to improve your performance, even without ever reaching perfection, because standards are rising all the time. The best thing is to compete with your own personal standard, which you will naturally raise as your performance level increases.

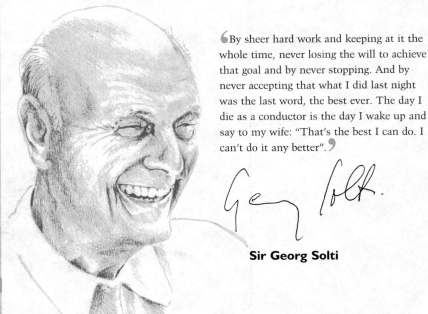

❝By sheer hard work and keeping at it the whole time, never losing the will to achieve that goal and by never stopping. And by never accepting that what I did last night was the last word, the best ever. The day I die as a conductor is the day I wake up and say to my wife: "That's the best I can do. I can't do it any better".❞

**Sir Georg Solti**

# Introduction

Measures of success in business are invariably obvious and/or predetermined by corporate or financial criteria. Managers will, therefore, understand their working environment, why and when they receive rewards for good performance and, conversely, why they get fired. For performing musicians, there are also identifiable criteria for success and perhaps even more identifiable criteria for failure! Performing musicians, be they soloists or orchestral players, are usually more aware of their weaknesses than their strengths - they are always self-critical.

For conductors, the measures of success, given that they do not play a note, are less clear - either to themselves or to the critics and audiences. Curiously, many orchestral players will form immediate and permanent impressions of new conductors and will deem them 'successes' or 'failures' - with equal arbitrariness. How, therefore, can a conductor measure his or her own success and how can they, therefore, maintain it? For conductors, success is often in the eye of the beholder, and can often remain elusive for decades and suddenly, for no obvious reason other than fad or fashion, become manifest. Often it can be the mere longevity, or staying power, of a conductor that will bring the final reward - when nothing in the conductor's musicianship has changed in any way. At other times, success can come with a major recording, or prestigious orchestral appointment but, these days, rarely with a single memorable concert performance. In recent years, only Daniele Gatti, with his remarkable performance of Mahler 6 with the New York Philharmonic Orchestra, has had his career transformed by one single concert event.

Clearly, success for a conductor can be either external, ie: critical acclaim and consequent high fees, or internal, ie: the feeling of great music-making having been achieved, by the conductor's own criteria. All conductors acknowledge that success can only come to them with the help of their orchestras and for this they need to be able to develop very special human and working relationships. In that sense, they are very 'modern' managers; gone, by and large, is the era of the great orchestral autocrats - the Mravinskys, the Toscaninis, the Karajans - and in their place have evolved a cadre of highly professional team leaders who tease and motivate, who form the most creative and complex of partnerships, who inspire and direct and who stand or fall by other people's judgement. No easy task and, while there are few managers who could take this level of personal risk on a daily basis, there are many who think they can. There is no equivalent of the Harvard Business School for conductors, but perhaps conductors could be usefully employed by such institutions for, as this book has shown, many of the requisite talents are common.

**John Manger**

# How To Stay Successful

In a team, the personal standard of performance has to be adopted collectively so that all members support and supplement each other. Andrew Litton describes the force of teamwork as the collective combination of knowledge, experience and different behaviour enabling the team to achieve things that nobody would think possible.

Both conductor and business leader are facilitators of that force. Another key success factor is the ability to channel the energy of employees towards reaching the goals.

*When I was starting out my conducting career, I was conducting my first children's concert for the orchestra and the door of my dressing room swung open with a bang and in walked one of the violinists from the National Symphony. She pointed a finger at me - she was a formidable, large woman - and she said: "You! You're good. But just don't ever forget that the collective knowledge and experience of everyone on stage is far greater than yours will ever be." And she turned on her heels and walked out of the room. I just sat there shaking for about half an hour! Obviously 100 people are going to have more collective knowledge and experience than one. Where a great conductor comes into being is when he knows where to channel all that collective knowledge and experience into a collective whole, into something that will ultimately make great music.*

**Andrew Litton**

*I think the conductor should be the man with the
musical soul which is as broad as possible, having
swallowed the music himself and then letting the musicians eat
and enjoy this great meal with him. Every time I do a concert
with no matter what orchestra, especially mine, I know there are
things which lie dormant in people which need to be awoken.
And after a performance which is great, they think: "Wow! That
was something within me! I didn't know that!" This is
another of my aims - to make musicians reach up
to another level of their abilities.*

**Christoph Eschenbach**

*Success as a conductor has nothing
to do with movement. It has everything to do
with the persona, the personality and a person's
ability to communicate with the musicians and convey your
ideas. The strength of the performance comes in conveying your
involvement in the process, rather than being a god who wields
the whip with the capacity to open and close the door. You must
be someone who embraces and helps the orchestra. The most
effective leadership, to me, is the leadership that doesn't look like
leadership. The moment somebody walks in looking and
sounding like a 'leader', that's quite suspicious to me. You must
be part of the process - so convinced by what you are doing that
everyone else has no choice but to follow you. It's intuition and
personality. You have to encourage people to open up, seduce
them, not scare them, to follow you.
That's a great leader.*

**Paavo Järvi**

*As a player, I was with the LSO, which has always been regarded as the second best orchestra in London. Then Stokowski was persuaded to come and work with the LSO and in about three days he managed to transmit to us the notion that we were a great orchestra. It gave us enormous confidence and we suddenly realised, in one concert at the Festival Hall, that we could achieve, had just achieved, a great performance - that we could achieve it just as easily as any other orchestra in the world. I think it was a great turning point for the orchestra suddenly to be given this confidence in one performance. From that moment the LSO never looked back - it was extraordinary. What did he do? He put more responsibility on the players than they had before. He more or less said to them: "This is your orchestra and if you want it to be good then you must perform. I will do my best to make it happen but the responsibility is yours." He just had this remarkable ability to focus the emotion of an entire orchestra. His personality was immensely strong.*

**Sir Neville Marriner**

*Personally I may be a bit of a pessimist but when I'm on stage with my colleagues I try to be an optimist. Being able to channel that is one step on the way to having the ability to lead others. Save the pessimism for yourself.*

**Andrew Litton**

# How To Stay Successful

> *You do need to carry on a dialogue within your personality. Otherwise one part of it will somehow be shrinking, and that's bad.*

**Christoph von Dohnányi**

> *The main thing is, you have to love yourself. Until you love yourself, you can't really love anyone else. Know yourself, accept yourself, be yourself. We were brought up with this. It's Plato. "Iona, if you take the mirror away the view is very pleasant. On the other hand, you have to look inside. When did you last take out your personality and have a really good look?" They were tough, my parents.*

**Iona Brown**

> *One very basic truth about my craft is that you must have a certain self-assurance or else you can't stand up on that box and tell people what to do. So there is some denial in admitting you could be wrong. You must really believe in what you do. If there's any sense of insecurity or of hedging, your colleagues on stage will be the first to dismiss you. Finding the balance where you can be true to yourself and not just an arrogant pig is very tough and again something you evolve over a long period of time.*

**Andrew Litton**

*The most important quality to have is musicality – it is vital that the players respect you as a musician. The second most important quality is determination. People say I am easy-going, but underneath I am extremely determined to have the piece played the way I conceive of it. In order to achieve this successfully you have to be able to judge the moood of the orchestra, and this is dependent partly on instinct and partly on experience.*

**Richard Hickox**

# How To Stay Successful

*Success as a conductor has to do with the exchange of radiation between the conductor and the orchestra. It must be that. There is no formula to being a conductor. That's why I won't teach it. What works for me doesn't necessarily work for the next man. You can learn a few basic technical things about conducting, but that's all. But after that, it's up to you. No amount of best practices will get you a performance, without (and you're not allowed to use these words anymore) the spiritual input, you're not going to get anything.*

**Sir Colin Davis**

*One of the jobs of a conductor is to give the players maximum confidence, to feel free. In order to get that you have to have such discipline - that is, the conductor as well as the players. That sounds like a contradiction in terms, that on the one hand you have to have the discipline and on the other you have to have the courage to take risks - controlled risks.*

**Iona Brown**

*There is a certain security in being in an environment in which you know how to deal with your tasks and you know what it takes to do them well. You can be most out of control only when you are completely secure. People who let themselves get completely out of control actually have the most control. I mean, it's only the people who are secure in knowing that they have something to fall back on who can allow themselves to be completely out of control.*

**Paavo Järvi**

*When things are going well you've got your audience with you. It's all to do with something up here, you see. I don't really believe in telepathy, but something communicates itself. This two-way street between the audience and the performers is so important. When they feel they are taking part in something special it snowballs. You start off with silence and it's like a heartbeat.*

**Iona Brown**

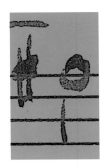

# Knowing When To Change

Proactiveness in leadership includes the ability to sense when it is right to change. Where do you find the pointers that help you to reach the right conclusion? It's a matter of interpreting signals in your team as well as in your customers.

You may need to analyse carefully data on trends in your area of business in order to spot the first changes in the market before anyone else. The same applies to your team; you must be able to respond to any change in their support with changes in your own conduct. This will regenerate trust and enthusiasm.

In our profession you have to try to find an inner equilibrium which prevents you from being tense all the time. Today, for instance, the rehearsal was an hour and a half late in starting and I had to try to re-arrange the whole thing. Twenty years ago I would have been very tense, but now I just tell myself that it doesn't make sense to shout and look for confrontation. So you reflect and say: "What is the best alternative?" So I decided the best thing to do was to make a lot of music with the minimum interruption.

**Christoph von Dohnányi**

The most important thing about leadership is how you comport yourself in front of an orchestra, maintaining one's calm and composure in front of a group. How to bring out the best of every individual within the group is, of course, a difficult thing. It has to do essentially with learning to be patient, showing respect. When I'm unhappy with myself, for example, when I'm not convinced that what I'm doing is effective, those are the moments when I'm the most fragile, when I can be negative towards the group. That's bad. It's something I'm still learning to control.

**William Christie**

95

*When I find myself saying the same things in front of an orchestra or an audience or in front of my students it's time to change. Or when I'm not deriving the kind of personal pleasure that I think I should be deriving. I have certain repertoires which I love to return to over and over again, to re-think them. But when I feel I have nothing else to say, that's the time for change.*

**William Christie**

An open attitude which embraces change should always be there and that way you will often discover new things. Honesty to yourself is also important. Music and art are the mirror of your insight. If you have made up your mind to change you have the force of conviction within you. You have reflected and projected and it is understood why change may be necessary.

**Christoph Eschenbach**

As you know, the whole business of performance has to do with the chemistry of the people involved. You can sense from what is essentially a team the degree of satisfaction they have had - emotional satisfaction, technical satisfaction - from the performance. But there is undoubtedly a frisson of excitement in the air which is sadly missing in other performances when you have not achieved that spectacular result. Now why it happens on some occasions and not others one doesn't know - it's just that it suddenly affects them. It catches their emotions or their intellect, whatever you are appealing to, and you know then that you have either hit or missed.

**Sir Neville Marriner**

# Tips On How To Stay Successful

Let's sum up the conductors' reflections relevant to leadership challenges in business:

- Play the inner strings of people - they are always there ready to be awakened and used.

- Be an optimist in front of your team, save the pessimism for yourself.

- Build up the confidence of the team by putting responsibility on the members and focus the emotion and energy of the entire team towards a clear, but ambitious goal.

- Take care of your own development as a leader and have a look at your personality. You may find something to be proud of or to adjust!

- Believe in yourself, your mission and your competence without becoming arrogant. In other words, share your passion and make your team members share your own experience.

- Read the group and judge the mood.

- Keep an open attitude; this is a basis for new insight and for renewal.

- Master the different processes of leadership: instil discipline and give freedom within a framework to align all forces in the right direction. Add sharing the passion and energy, and you have a simple leadership model.

# The Passion Model

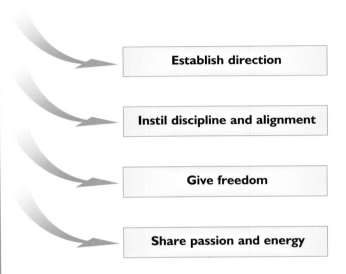

The model summarises the essence of the total leadership experience presented in this book. Establishment of purpose and direction will enable team members to understand their effort in relation to the greater picture: what are we doing and why?

Instilling discipline and alignment by principles and values will establish the framework you need in order to go further and give freedom. You may find the contradiction seemingly uncomfortable, giving freedom and at the same time establishing a framework to control that freedom. However, life is full of contradictions like that: we need both rain and sun, happiness and sorrow, and people need both freedom and structure.

During the last decade delegation has been one of the most frequently described strategies in management literature. Our model comprises that strategy in relation to giving freedom to choose work tools and mode of performance. Freedom increases creativity and motivation, but teams and organisations will need a framework to ensure that human energy is channelled in the desired direction.

So far you have built the most fruitful platform for high performance in teamwork. To add that next step and break down the limits of your mind to reach radical improvement of team performance, you will need to share your own passion for the purpose with your team members. They have to own **your** passion and live by it. For a team possessing qualities like that everything is possible!

# Acknowledgements

This project would have stayed a dream had it not been for the willingness and interest of the conductors to share their philosophy and experience with me. Making me able to share it with you, I want to thank and salute them all: Sir Colin Davis, Iona Brown, Sir Neville Marriner, Richard Hickox, William Christie, Paavo Järvi, Neeme Järvi, Andrew Litton, Christoph Eschenbach, Jane Glover, David Atherton, Sir Georg Solti, Daniele Gatti, Philippe Herreweghe and Christoph von Dohnányi.

Approaching world class conductors constantly on the road between the concert halls of the world is not an easy task. It would have been next to impossible without the help and assistance I received from the music agencies of London. I am grateful to several people in the following agencies: Harold Holt, Harrison Parrot, IMG Artists, Lies Askonas, Inter Musica and Columbia Artists. Thanks also to Alison Glaister, the secretary of Sir Colin Davis, and Charles Kaye, secretary and companion of Sir Georg Solti, who supplied me with invaluable information and insight.

I am grateful to the administration of the Orchestre des Champs Elysées La Chapelle Royale, Paris, the Academy of Saint Martin in the Fields, The Royal Philharmonic Orchestra, and the London Symphony Orchestra (LSO), London, as well as to some of the players in the LSO for useful background information and their sharing of experiences on working with world class conductors.

I had a useful afternoon tea with writer and critic Norman Lebrecht as I started my search for the conductors. He inspired me and gave me useful tips.

I wanted the introductions to be written by businessmen with one foot in business and one in music. A managing director of one of the world's most famous symphony orchestras, a managing director of one of the world's most famous concert and art centres, and the chairman of a recognised global business company would make the perfect balance for introductions to the theme. I am very grateful to John Tusa of the Barbican Centre, John Manger of the Royal Philharmonic Orchestra and Helmut Maucher of Nestlé for their focused and insightful introductions to the book.

Last, but not least, I want to thank Ros Baynes, Management Pocketbooks, for believing in my project from the day I presented my idea.

**Jan R. Jonassen**
Stavanger, Norway
September 1998

**Phillip Hailstone's** original drawings based on photographs of the conductors.
Sources, where known, are as follows:

**Sir Colin Davis** - Michael Powell, **Christoph Eschenbach and Andrew Litton** - Steve Sherman,
**Paavo Järvi** - David Harrison, **Richard Hickox** - Nigel Luckhurst, **Christoph von Dohnányi** - Terry O'Neil/Decca,
**Iona Brown** - Suzie E Maeder, **William Christie** - Michael Szabo, **David Atherton** - Hong Kong Philharmonic,
**Jane Glover** - Mirror Australian Telegraph Publications.

# The Participants

**Sir Colin Davis,** since 1975 principal guest conductor of the London Symphony Orchestra.

**Iona Brown,** since 1974 artistic director of the Academy of Saint Martin in the Fields, London, and since 1981 music and artistic director of the Norwegian Chamber Orchestra, Oslo. Since 1987 music director of the Los Angeles Chamber Orchestra and chief conductor of the South Jutland Orchestra, from 1996.

**Sir Neville Marriner,** founder and musical director of the Academy of Saint Martin in the Fields, London, since 1959.

**Richard Hickox,** principal conductor of the London Symphony Chorus and musical director of the London Sinfonia.

**William Christie,** founder of Les Arts Florissants, Paris.

**Neeme Järvi,** chief conductor of the Gothenburg Symphony Orchestra from 1982, and music director of the Detroit Symphony Orchestra since 1990.

**Paavo Järvi,** son of Neeme, principal guest conductor with the Royal Stockholm Philharmonic Orchestra, the City of Birmingham Symphony Orchestra and Norden Youth Orchestra.

**Andrew Litton,** music director of the Dallas Symphony Orchestra, since 1994, and principal guest conductor of the Bournemouth Symphony Orchestra since 1986.

**Christoph Eschenbach,** music director of The Houston Symphony, since 1988.

**Christoph von Dohnányi,** music director of the Pittsburgh Symphony Orchestra.

**Jane Glover,** did some major productions at the time of the interviews, Glimmerglass Productions, Glimmerglass, New York City Opera and Opéra de Bordeaux.

**David Atherton,** co-founder and musical director of the London Sinfonietta since 1967. Principal guest conductor of the BBC National Orchestra of Wales.

**Sir Georg Solti,** one of the most celebrated conductors in the world. He appeared regularly as guest conductor with the great orchestras of the world. Sadly, he died in September 1997.

**Daniele Gatti,** musical director of the Royal Philharmonic Orchestra, London, since 1996. Principal guest conductor of the Royal Opera House Orchestra, Covent Garden, London.

**Philippe Herreweghe,** artistic director of the Orchestre des Champs Elysées La Chapelle Royale, Paris.

*All of these conductors appear regularly as guest conductors with the great orchestras of the world.*

*The biographical data reflects the situation at the time of the interviews during 1997.*

# The Management Pocketbook Series

## Pocketbooks

Appraisals Pocketbook

Assertiveness Pocketbook

Balance Sheet Pocketbook

Business Planning Pocketbook

Business Presenter's Pocketbook

Business Writing Pocketbook

Challengers Pocketbook

Coaching Pocketbook

Communicator's Pocketbook

Creative Manager's Pocketbook

Cultural Gaffes Pocketbook

Customer Service Pocketbook

Empowerment Pocketbook

Export Pocketbook

Facilitator's Pocketbook

Improving Profitability Pocketbook

Interviewer's Pocketbook

Key Account Manager's Pocketbook

Learner's Pocketbook

Manager's Pocketbook

Manager's Training Pocketbook

Managing Budgets Pocketbook

Managing Cashflow Pocketbook

Managing Change Pocketbook

Managing Your Appraisal Pocketbook

Marketing Pocketbook

Meetings Pocketbook

Mentoring Pocketbook

Motivation Pocketbook

Negotiator's Pocketbook

People Manager's Pocketbook

Performance Management Pocketbook

Project Management Pocketbook

Quality Pocketbook

Sales Excellence Pocketbook

Salesperson's Pocketbook

Self-managed Development Pocketbook

Stress Pocketbook

Teamworking Pocketbook

Telephone Skills Pocketbook

Telesales Pocketbook

Thinker's Pocketbook

Time Management Pocketbook

Trainer Standards Pocketbook

Trainer's Pocketbook

## Pocketfiles

Trainer's Blue Pocketfile of

Ready-to-use Exercises

Trainer's Green Pocketfile of

Ready-to-use Exercises

Trainer's Red Pocketfile of

Ready-to-use Exercises

## Audio Cassettes

Tips for Presenters

Tips for Trainers

## Other Titles

The Great Presentation Scandal

# About the Author

Jan R. Jonassen, BA., MA., has been Chief Executive of SiR, one of Norway's biggest hospitals, since 1997. He has 20 years' experience gained in leadership positions in public agencies and companies, and from leadership and organisational development as a consultant to European international corporations. During his nine years (1988-1997) as a consultant, mostly for The Performance Group, Oslo and London, he was the author or co-author of several books/reports based on field studies among top leaders in national or international business. The major international work in that respect was 'The Gateway to High Performance', *1994, The Performance Group*, a study based on interviews with successful leaders in various walks of life, aiming to describe a model for reaching high performance in leadership. During his stay in London (1994-1997) he was responsible for designing a training programme for building teamwork in international corporations. He has been a speaker at national and international conferences on leadership and productivity.

# Order Form